Disclaimer: This book is based on true events. However, any depictions of names, characters, places, and religious affiliations, etc. are entirely fictional. The author is not responsible for any outside opinions and/or actions.

From Alef to Beth

From Alef to Beth

Master
Ayen Jewels

FROM ALEF TO BETH.

First published in The United States of America, 2013.

ISBN: 978-1-304-35838-7

This book is dedicated to the entire human race. If there was any dream to do to prove that dreams could come true, may I suggest this dream to you. These types of dreams are only provable by you, in hopes you will be curious. If you ever want to dream together, the next turn goes to you.
If you ever forget you're special, do know that I love you. Unconditionally.

~~~

Thanks for reading.
I hope you enjoy my dreaming.
~~~

Acknowledgments

I would like to thank my friends and all the people I have met for helping me learn and grow into a better person.
I would like to thank my family for their support and kindness towards me. Thanksgiving is my favorite holiday.
I would like to thank my Mom for always believing in me.
I would like to thank my Dad for always challenging and supporting my apprenticeship program.
I would like to thank all my lovers. As those who get the closest to me, each of you have inspired my heart.
I will always love you.

~~~

Laus Deo.
Thank you most of all.
~~~

Prologue

I am a fool. These are my follies.

Initiation

I was seventeen years young and dating a girl who was white as porcelain; we both knew she would glow in the dark if held to the light long enough beforehand.

We were at her parents' house, a massive concrete igloo in the country side. Her father had prepared for the deadliest of weather or a nuclear attack – if necessary. Dense, gray vines climbed trestles and wound around the exterior, while various shrubs and garden flowers colored the ground below. It was a wonderland. We spent a lot of time together there, but this time was different.

Jacob was his name. He visited, as friends to both of us, and we got along well. Jacob was a Pagan. I was agnostic. I never had a definitive answer, but I do now, and by the end of this book, I hope you also have the curiosity to figure it out for yourself.

Jacob said he could make the wind blow.

"Really?" I asked, hoping it were true.

"Yeah," he confirmed. "It just takes some concentration. That bad storm last week? That wasn't me, that was Sam." She was another Pagan follower. I knew about her, but didn't *know* her. You know what I mean.

"Wow," I lied. "That's cool."

"...Can you do it now?" I challenged.

We went outside to the front porch. Jacob sat down cross-legged on the wood and closed his eyes. A few minutes passed and the wind blew. It was absolutely... normal. It was disappointing. There was nothing impressive about it. I didn't show it though. When the wind blew, Jacob was modest and said it was all he could do. If he wanted to do more, it would have required more time and "energy."

I asked about what this "energy" was and he told me it was the aura: a bio-luminescent field that surrounds every object, whether alive or not. He proceeded to show me how to feel my aura. He formed the shape of a pistol with his right hand, opened his left palm and instructed me to do the same. He pointed the finger gun at his open palm and slowly circled the gun towards his hand. I followed along and, as I moved my hands closer, I felt a circle forming in my palm. My hands never touched. He told me the circling sensation was the reaction of my aura. The trick worked, but I dismissed it and figured I was just feeling static electricity. I was wrong.

The next day, I left my house and took a walk to the store. It was a nice day: warm, partly cloudy, normal – nothing outstanding. I purchased a carbonated beverage and was nearing my home when I decided to try it.

The Calling

Walking back from the store, I formed my right hand into a pistol shape and opened my left. I pointed the fingernail barrel at my palm and started turning. I could feel the electricity instantly.

I flattened my hands out and placed them side by side, as if rolling a meatball. I started rolling, slowly letting the movement hypnotize me. I began staring at my palms, picturing lightning bolts jumping back and forth between the gap in my hands. The electric charge grew stronger. As I continued to imagine rolling the lightning into a ball, I could feel the resistance and charge expanding. It wanted to grow.

I started spreading it out, stretching it apart like a cluster of rubber bands stuck in a ball of glue. My imagination was absolute and focused. There was an electric lightning ball glowing in my hands.

I kept going until it reached the size of a basketball.

W*hat the hell do I do with this?* I said to myself, breaking focus.

I tossed it up towards the clouds. *It's gone now.*

It took a few seconds before I noticed. Giant, wet circles crashed to the pavement around me. It was raining.

Did I do this?

The rain fell for a minute's time before ceasing, but it was a minute of absolute confusion. I was frightened.

The Fool

When I was in elementary school, I was bullied. I wasn't very modern – I didn't know the lyrics to all the songs on the radio and my clothes were queer, but I was smart and I didn't care. It was quite humbling, socially.

I befriended my friendliest and most forgiving abuser, Jeremiah, and remained his friend throughout time. We worked together in aspirations and games. He has a tattoo written around his collar: *'No Man, Nor God, Can Bind Me.'*

I don't think it's true because he's always been with me.

It was high school, freshman year. Jeremiah was a practicing Satanist at the time. He read the book by Anton LaVey; didn't believe in the magic rituals or the selling of the soul crap, but he took note in the message of personal power. A Satanist's main goal is to attain ultimate earthly rewards. It isn't a journey of spirit, but of body. That's why Satanism gets the rapport it does. Many other religions function towards attaining spiritual power – the reward after death. Satanism is the opposite, superiority during life.

"Energy is neither created, nor destroyed, but merely transformed." Try to remember it because it makes death better. It is a common statement in physics, which also applies to religion in this matter. Both religious perceptions are differing beliefs about the transference of energy. Neither is wrong, but one is notably more righteous than the other.

Jeremiah and I had been friends for many years without any conflicts. We were brothers from other mothers and our friends knew it.

One day, I walked down the stairs and turned the corner to all of our friends staring at me, mouths agape, just mystified. Jeremiah had a big grin on his face.

One of them chimed up and said to me, “Jeremiah said you were coming, and, a few seconds later, you walked down the stairs.”

“Yep,” I laughed. “We're psychic.”

~~~

Skipping to the future: High school is over. My adolescent mischief was boring and the time to grow into an adult was bearing down. I denied it. I drank tequila with an empty stomach, ate painkillers like they were candy, and smoked a chain of cigarettes with enough marijuana hits to stone Pancho Villa and all the horses he rode in on. I never let it get out of control, but I was never in control, either.

I stole, lied and cheated my way through relationships. I betrayed few friends, but lost more to selfish ignorance. I condemned my enemies and cut them down from the inside out if they attacked me. I used my studies as a weapon. I was clever when persuasion was dangerous.

~~~

I had a wonderful woman during my fall. She was a sunflower. We were together for a few years after my fall from grace. I was powerless, but I knew I had beauty in me. Deep down, I could feel it and she knew it too. I felt so empowered around her, it made me guilty. She was the pin cushion for my shame. As she grew closer, I pushed her away.

From her, I discovered the learned helplessness of a soul. She was beautiful and extraordinarily talented, but always held herself back. Afraid to follow her dreams, she sunk into them through intravenous means and I lost her forever.

Without her to ground me, I floated off into space. I spent many hours a day, for months at a time, in a drugged haze, stumbling through my interests on the web: quantum mechanics, spirituality, ghosts and the paranormal, astral projection, the pyramids, aliens and all the other eccentric mysteries.

I was absolutely lost, until one day.

"Hey. You want to burn one?" It was my Dad.

Up In Smoke

The long-stemmed pipe looked like a prop from J.R.R. Tolkien's *The Lord of the Rings* books. Dad pulled a match and lit a corner of the green herb on fire. The orange ember burned across the small forest before being extinguished through a vacuum. I took the pipe and inhaled the smoke. It was a delicious treat, a taste that only long-stem pipes can deliver. The effect is even better.

"Sometimes, when you smoke me up, it's hard to keep my eyes open." The space between my brows vibrated with pressure, like God himself was pressing his thumb against my brain.

"Yep. You don't need to see at that level," he said.

"What does that mean?" I asked.

"This world is an illusion, fake, like an imaginary figment of some common sense." *What?* He then quoted a lyric from a song, "there is no fucking you, there is only me."

"So, who is there?" I asked.

"Nobody is there. There is nobody, only me. I make my own reality."

"Just you?"

"It's all the common sense. What you see is what we all see," he claimed. "It's not about what you see, but how you look. It's like *The Matrix* movies. Those guys, the Wacha-chao – whatever brothers, they stumbled onto some truth with that."

"Yeah? So you're the only one here?" I was still stuck.

"Reality is just an illusion. Everyone you meet is like a mirror of yourself. There is no fucking you, there is only me!"

That didn't help at all, but he continued.

"It's all about personal power – the ability to stop time. I practice it when I go to the gas station. I picture my car sitting there in the space and it'll be open when I get there – just for me." He smiled. "That's one of the ways of collecting personal power. Good deeds and stuff, ya know, they give you power too."

What kind of power?

Inter Net

This is my home. I live on the Internet, stumbling all I can on the invention of life: learning about sacred geometry and its connection to the quantum mechanics of Genesis; to the notoriously aware photon, whose knot is still entangled to this day by acting, both, like a particle and a wave; into black holes and out through gamma rays, down to the X-ray spectrum, to cooking in microwaves. I studied little bits of it all; from rectifying granite, to Thor's old, mighty hammer – I researched this delusion and now I can't manage. At this moment, this is where I am: stuck in the Internet, with my ideas as wings, floating around wondering, waiting.

Would you hear my whistles or will I just blow away?

Convincidences

A convincidence is an incidence in reality convincing enough to prove that reality is more unreal than we think.

I practiced Dad's gas station manipulation trick, but I decided to take it a step further. I pictured the station in my mind and called out loud, "Okay, white car and red van: please move. I'm coming to get gas." A moment later, I was driving down a hill. The gas station was in sight. A white car was sitting in my spot. As I drove closer, its lights turned on and the car pulled away. A gray car was parked behind it, also blocking my spot. As I neared the entrance, the gray car flicked on. I pulled in and the car drove away, leaving the spot I wanted open – just for me. I parked, turned off my car and thought: *Where's the red van?*

I looked to my left and there it was: across the lot, pumping gas.

~~~

Just recently, during the September – October 2012 McDonald's monopoly game, I made a wish to receive a large sum of money before going to sleep. The next day my friend called me and said his uncle has the winning piece: Boardwalk. Knowing I had Park Place, he suggested we split it three ways. *What?!*

As it turned out, it was a mistake and his uncle did not have the winning piece, but I felt like a million dollars anyway.

~~~

I went to a gas station one day and, for some reason, I had the feeling to buy a scratch ticket. I rarely gamble, but I took the chance on a single cheap ticket. I handed the kind, elderly clerk a ten-dollar bill and told her, with confidence, that I'll be back.

Sure enough, I scratched the ticket, returned to the store, and won my ten-dollar bill back.

~~~

I went outside one night and looked at the stars. I found a bright one and was immediately astounded.

"Hello bright star." I called out to it.

It dimmed, slowly, and swelled to its full brightness. It dimmed again, and swelled to its full brightness before twinkling like a normal star. *Hel-lo.*

~~~

I was hanging out with a friend of mine. We were talking about the weird occurrences of reality, such as the examples in this chapter. The conversation moved to myths of the apocalypse and what was going to happen at the end of the world. We were leaving to go somewhere in the car. I turned the key over in the ignition and the radio hummed on. Blasting from the speakers was a familiar tune. "It's the end of the world as we know it! It's the end of the world as we know it... and I feel fine!"

I looked at him with and grin and said, "That's how it works."

~~~

One day, I was reading about these cloud beings
~~~

called *Sylphs*. I thought it pleasant to think of clouds as living beings. A couple of days passed and I went out back to burn some trash. I looked up at the sky, and floating by went two identical clouds, both with faces and bodies like outstretched wings – observing me as I watched them. It was quite odd.

~~~

The Celtics were down eighteen points. They called a time out. It was the last five minutes of the game, so the advertisers took advantage and cut to a commercial. I closed my eyes and wished for the Celtics to win. I repeated it in my head until the commercials ended. The players returned to the court. Game on.

In three minutes, the Celtics shutout the opposing team and brought their trail of eighteen down to three. I was buzzing with excitement. The other coach called a time out and the game cut to a commercial. After, the ball went to the other team. They scored two points, Celtics down by five. Another time out was called, followed by a routine commercial. By this time, the buzz was gone. The Celtics managed to stay close, but couldn't overcome and lost.

~~~

I opened the door and let my cat inside. It went, “mew mew.” I heard *thank you*.

~~~

A teacher once said to me that I was, “some kind of genius.” This, I didn't take lightly. I thanked him, secretly astounded. A college professor, a doctor and master of
~~~

professional education, had called me a genius! I didn't understand.

Charlie came over one night. She is clairvoyant in her dreams, but blind when she's awake. I try to help her see, but I can't, so it's just funny. We were together one night and she was staring at my door for no reason.

"What are you staring at?" I asked.

She glanced away and looked at me, "a speck of light."

"Come on out bro," I said to the door with a smile. I couldn't see it.

"It's above your head now." I looked up. I still couldn't see it.

A few days later, I heard a thought whisper by, "genie us."

~~~

My grandfather gave me a guitar he found in the trash somewhere. It was slightly cracked, but certainly playable, so I put strings on it and tuned her up. I always brought her to college, but only used a couple of times. I usually played the school piano for practice. I sat on the bench and lifted up the covering for the keys when a young man, skin black as night, walked in with his eyes set on it. He looked up at me.

"Hello," I said. "You can play. I don't mind," I stood up.

"No, no, no. You were here first," he replied, gesturing in defense.

"It's okay. I play it all the time," I said and left the bench.

I motioned for him to sit down. He did.

"What's your name?" I asked.
~~~

"Francis," he said playing a few nervous notes.

"How long have you been playing?"

"Not very long," he answered ringing his fingers around on the piano again, but quickly stood up.

He beckoned for me to sit down, so I did. I played the only song I knew.

He smiled. "That's awesome."

"Thanks. My only secret: don't hit the black keys."

He laughed.

"Do you play any other instruments?" I asked him.

"No, but I wished I played guitar."

"Well, your wish is my command!" I led him out to my car and gave him the guitar that had slammed around in the trunk for months.

~~~

For the past four years now, I have wished for world peace and harmony. At 11:11, I would close my eyes and whisper with the silent voice in my head: *I wish for world peace and harmony.* I called this my personal wish-craft.

I took it farther when it started to come true. I'm a musician with many songs waiting in my head. I participated in a vocal competition once, but there were only two other competitors and they were both awesome, so I never returned. After I sang, I looked out at the woman who sung before me. She smiled and whistled adoration through her fingers. I formed a heart with my hands and put it on my chest as a thank you. I still practice my songs and continue to write them, but I'm afraid to play them. I like to save them for my lovers.

My wish for harmony came true. World peace, however, that is a wish best left up to you, but I'm here to serve, if you want to see all the work I can do.
~~~

Dreaming

My friends were noticing the quarrels of the world. Along with myself, we were feeling the drag of work and the restrictions and responsibilities a lack of money brought. My friends always had a debt. They left their nests and bought new cars, apartments and houses. I didn't. I stayed home and saved my money. I had everything, but myself. I wanted to earn that identity.

We noticed the world was getting weak. The American people were losing out on the American dream. By choosing debts towards an empty future, their job stresses grew and their paychecks lacked fuel.

Jeremiah had a kid and his life went a new direction, away from me.

With that, they left, and I grew faint. A whisper in their hearts, I remained. I was a childhood character and they were growing up. I knew my path had to take me back, so I had to give them up. I worked with children who had special needs. These kids could often dream like me, but their brains were so vexed, they couldn't see. It was a metaphor. I was awake, but pretending to sleep.

Black Holes

Plato once said that witnessing reality is like being chained to a chair in a cave. There is a light, but it's behind us, so the reality we perceive are just the shadows of reality. Plato then suggested that the philosopher is a man who can break away the chains, can stand up to face the light able to see the objects and shapes, to walk towards the source and yell back to the others, "This is what I see!"

I stayed home and collected my thoughts. I burned through the Internet for clues. I looked at the natural world for truth.

The environment was being destroyed by my own species. Uncontrolled, I ran through the conspiracy theories, assassinations, government lies and cover-ups, forbidden technology, medicine, psychology, energy, politics, war and money. I was disgusted.

Then, one day after a wish, I heard it.

Har-money.

Har! Money! Kill money! Rip up the root of all evil! However, as we covered earlier, energy can neither be created nor destroyed, merely transformed.

I thought about how to facilitate a worthless economy based on compassion and sustainability, the greater good and the progress of knowledge and art. I spent months walking back and forth through my bedroom, sizing up my enemy – money – and how it works. I cut it into pieces and simplified it to an equation. I built a system of limitless progress with infinite motivation.

It was governed by Justice, founded on Democracy, debated through a Republic and stapled with Love. I knew no one would believe me. Even if they did, they wouldn't think the same of me again. I never stopped believing I could change the world.

~~~

I have to take a leap of faith.

I started buying stuff and making plans. My dream fueled the motivation as curiosity steered me along. I even bought a pair of cowboy boots to protect me from poisonous, ankle-biting snakes. I bought a cowboy hat, too, for consistency.

I heard three whistles, one after another, break through the air. It was Dad.

I came out of my room.

"Wanna burn one?" He asked.

"Sure," I answered. I grabbed a piece of paper and headed downstairs. I was going to tell him my plan.

He led me out to the porch and lit the pipe.

I started talking about my wish to make money worthless and find a new way to arrange the government to accommodate it. My hands shook as I drew out the general ideas in circles and they branched up like a tree. From the stem of democracy, to social awareness, to a more interactive government, the idea grew on paper in front of Dad. Circled in the center was one word: Money.

"This isn't going to work." Dad stopped me before I could reach the top. "The world is too big, people aren't just going to do this," he paused, "but it's a good dream."

We kept smoking and I finished the tree. We talked about it some more and shared ideas, but he didn't see it happening here. He was right.

"Can you help me clean out the stuff under the porch next week?" Dad asked.

"I can't," I said. "I'll be gone."

"Where are you going?"

"To the Hopi Indian reservation."
~~~

"Oh," he paused.

"When?"

"Tomorrow." I had bought the ticket a week before.

"Tomorrow!" He didn't look mad.

"Yeah." I was sad. "I wanted to tell you, but I was afraid."

"Oh," he paused. "What's over there?"

"I don't know, really," I answered, truthfully. "They have the legends of spaceships, the "ships without wings." They might be able to communicate with them or something and help me with my plan. I don't know what I'll find, but I want to start looking and that's a good place to start."

"Well," he paused. "Be careful. Those places are worse than the ghetto."

"Really?" I asked, surprised.

"Yeah, they don't have any police or social structure down there, just... wild. They're a different culture, so they're imprisoned by diversity. They receive money from the government, but it doesn't help. It's just a different way of life down there."

"Wow," I said. "Not only did we steal their land, we stole their dreams."

"Well, they really couldn't compete with our growing culture. At least they weren't slaves."

He lit the pipe. The soft green burned from an orange into a fiery red. I inhaled the colors, absorbing their dyes, before releasing them together as a pale, gray cloud. The colors blended in my lungs and I coughed.

"Gotta cough to get off," he said as he finished off the herb, opened the door and led the way inside.

Flattened out on the pool table was a new painting Dad had bought. He was preparing to frame it. I looked down at the picture.

It was a desert scene. A spaceship was hovering in the sky above a cactus. From the ship shined a blue beam down onto a cowboy below. I couldn't believe what I was looking at. I didn't mention the convincidence to Dad. I didn't want to spoil the joy. *Thank you, Time Lord.*

That night, I vacuum shrunk all the dreams held in my pillow, packed my bags and jumped.

Leap of Faith

I flew through the air. The plane rumbled and took off as my internal organs lifted against gravity. It was a wild feeling. I looked out the window in amazement at the world fading below. *This is so beautiful.*

“Is this your first time?” The woman next to me asked. Her smile was pleasant and she wore glasses.

“Yeah,” I smiled.

“Oh, if I knew that, I would've given you the window seat.”

I chuckled. “Thanks. That's okay. It's beautiful anyways - amazing what we humans have accomplished. It really makes me excited about the future.” There was a pause.

“Where are you from?” She asked.

“The woods of Maine,” I replied. “You?”

She smiled. “I'm heading home to Phoenix. Are you going to Phoenix?” She asked.

“No. I'm going to Flagstaff to visit the Hopi Indians.”

“The Indians?”

“Yeah, they have legends about “ships without wings,” so I was wondering if I might be able to find one out there.”

“That's cool.” It was genuine. “Is it just you?”

“Yep, just me,” I said with confidence. “I even brought my cowboy boots just in case one of them desert snakes tries to bite me.”

She laughed. “That's funny. Well, I wish you luck.”

“Thanks.”

The steward reached us and chimed in. She asked if we wanted any beverages.

“I'll have a water. Thanks.”

Breaking the Chains

I landed in Flagstaff some hours after my flight. It was midnight in the west, but three in the morning back home. I took a taxi to the nearest hotel to rest for the night. I asked the driver about the natives and he said the locals that lived around town were nice, but he warned me to avoid the alcoholic ones and those asking for money.

It took a few minutes to get to the hotel. The taxi dropped me off. I couldn't wait to rest. I rented a room, took a shower and tried to sleep.

Tomorrow, I'll make my way into town and start exploring, I thought to myself.

That's exactly what I did. I established base at a motel downtown and spent the week drinking wine with a couple of Mexicans, exploring the small urban area. I planned it well; I'd rent a car on the upcoming Friday and spend as much time in the Hopi reservations as I could over the weekend.

Friday came and I had my stuff all packed. I left my bags at the motel and walked down to rent a car. They denied me for being too young and not having a proper credit card. It was a bad omen.

It was noon and I was running out of luck. I decided to check the college and ask the locals for help. I entered the circular culture building and asked a young man if he could help me get to the Hopi Reservations. When he asked why I was going to visit the natives, I declared myself as King Arthur with a plan to conquer America and I needed the blessings of the Hopi leaders. I had fun with it. He looked at me stunned for a moment, then brushed it off. He led me to another woman who printed out a brochure for a local bus route. I thanked them kindly and left.

The brochure read: **Only small items allowed on**

the bus.

Damn. I can't take my camping bag. Okay. The next route leaves at 3:15PM.

I looked at the clock on my cellphone: *2:13PM.*

I had an hour to throw a plan of action together.

I walked back to the motel to think. *45 minutes left.* I called a taxi to immediately pick me up. I left Epi, my guitar, and my camping equipment behind, in good faith the motel would keep it safe. I took a tea with me and waited for my ride.

The taxi arrived soon after. It was the same guy who had picked me up from my flight. He was quick and courteous; we made it there in time, but there was no bus. We waited a few minutes, to no avail, so I walked into a nearby restaurant and asked if they had seen it. They said it had already arrived minutes before, dropped a few people off and left. *Damn.*

I returned to the taxi and told the bad news. I asked how far it was to get there and an estimated cost.

"I'll take ya to Tuba City," he said. "It's right on the edge of the reservations."

"I'll buy it." I left my camping gear and guitar behind. *I'll miss you Epi.*

~~~

The taxi ride was nice. The driver had to bring his father along, due to conflicting schedules, but I had no problem with it. In the car we chatted about the locals, the changing environment and a few other things. We started talking about the drowning economy and such. I told the driver and his father the general idea of my dream and the curious mission I decided to take. They liked my passion, but I obviously had no direction. I was looking for one and they
~~~

could see that. The driver suggested that I call my travel a vision quest. I liked his definition.

After an hour-long ride, the taxi arrived at a gas station in Tuba City. I got out and took my bags from the trunk. The cab driver pointed me in the right direction. I said my thanks, goodbyes, and carried forth.

I had a liter of water and a can of tea to sustain me. The tea didn't last long. I got sick of carrying it, so I found the nearest dumpster, relaxed for a bit, and threw it in the garbage.

An hour of walking passed. Many cars had already went by, but I didn't need their help.

Another hour of walking and I had half a liter of water left. The sun was furious at me and I was getting nervous. There were no signs of civilization on the horizon. I saw a small bridge hundreds of feet up ahead.

If I have to, I'll just camp out under that bridge for the night.

I started making my way to the bridge when a white pickup pulled up.

“Hey. You need a ride?” The young man asked. He had short blonde hair. I moved closer to talk.

“Yeah!” I said excited. There was a passenger in the truck, a heavy, tan young man who certainly looked like a Native American. We all exchanged names.

“Hop in the back, man,” said the driver. I jumped in the rear of the pickup and took off my hat. The truck started to move. The breeze on my sweat soaked hair felt great.

“What are ya doin' out here?” The driver asked.

“I'm on a vision quest,” I replied, remembering what the taxi driver said to me.

They looked at me, befuddled, but accepting.

“A vision quest, uh? I like that.” The driver said. “That's cool.” A few minutes passed.

“You smoke weed?” He asked, breaking the silence.

“Of course!” He passed me the pipe. *This is a great start.*

~~~

“We're going to drop you off here. We can take you to the sun festival because we're going that way, but Oraibi is in the opposite direction.” The driver had taken me, at least, 30 miles from where he had picked me up.

“I really need to get closer to Oraibi. Is there anything there that could help? A hotel or something?” I had no camping equipment and needed to make a plan again.

“Yeah, there's a store near there.”

“Can you take me?” I pulled out my wallet and offered thirty dollars.

“Yeah, sure,” he agreed, “but don't let people see your money like that.”

“Why?” I asked.

“There are a lot of people here who would beat you to death and steal it,” he said. “You don't even know. What if we did?” He smiled, showing his humor about it.

“Well, you guys didn't seem like killers.”

We laughed and he drove me into town. I asked directions for a tourist hotel and he drove me there next. That's where we parted ways.

“I wish you luck, man. The world is going to Hell, even out here. Some days I wish for the zombie apocalypse. I'm preparin' and shit.” We laughed.

“You know,” I said. “The zombies are already here. They're the ones who don't believe in the spirit, that's why they're the living dead. They silence and kill those who speak up and share their belief. Why do you think they
~~~

want to eat your brains?" I laughed again, but it was an uncomfortable truth.

We shook hands, wished each other luck and parted ways.

The Cave

I spent the first night at the cultural center hotel planning for tomorrow. It was a nice place. There were a couple of beautiful, young native women that assisted customers. I gave them a lucky coin in exchange to see their eyes smile. I went to sleep early, but stayed asleep until noon.

There were no taxis and without a rental car, I had to walk to my destinations. The nearest store was six miles away.

That's okay. Oraibi is close by.

I started walking. I didn't hitch hike, I just walked with a song in my ear and a dance in my step. I nodded to all the cars that went by, a gesture of, *hello. I'm friendly. No harm, please.*

The store was a long walk, two and a half hours with a single liter of water. It was grotesquely hot as I neared the Kyokotsville store. A dog barked from the porch of a nearby house and I greeted the animal with a hello.

"Keep on walking," bellowed a voice from the porch. I ignored the rudeness, but obeyed and kept on.

The store was a few minutes from there, but it felt like an eternity. I was so glad to be around something familiar. I bought a few bottles of water and asked the clerk about Oraibi. She directed me towards the mesa and I left the store. I parked myself on the bench out front and relaxed for a minute.

~~~

"Hey brotha, how are ya?" I looked towards the voice. A dark Native American man, a little taller than me, was walking closer.
~~~

"Good. Yourself?" This is my naturally scripted response to a how are you, handed down from my father to me.

"Good. Whatcha got in the bag?" The man asked.

That question was invasive and I caught it. "Just some stuff."

"Where ya headed?"

"Oraibi."

"Oh yeah? We're going right there," he said. "Do you need a ride?"

"Umm," I pondered a moment too long. The man walked to a nearby truck, leaned into the window and asked the driver.

"Hey. Come with us. We'll take you," he said.

Okay. I plopped my bags down in the back and hopped into the cab. Two children greeted me with giggles and cheese crusted hands. I felt relieved to see them. They really liked my cowboy hat. The driver introduced himself as Martin and the man who offered the ride was named Arlen.

"We're going to take you to Walter's house, okay?" Martin said, shifting into gear and taking off.

"Okay. Is that near Oraibi?" I asked.

"Yeah, near it; right on the border of Hotevilla and Oraibi."

"Okay."

~~~

Walter's house was a small shack, no more than twenty square feet wide, made from cement blocks stacked up and sealed together to form the walls. He greeted us outside. He seemed like a friendly older man, but I could tell he was highly inebriated. He led us all into his house
~~~

and offered me a beer. I declined, so he gave it to Arlen.

"Whatcha got in the bag?" Arlen asked again, cracking open the beer.

I knew he meant harm. "I've got a hammock and some clothes."

"Oh yeah? You wanna go set that hammock up?" He took a gulp of his beer.

"No. I'm not staying here. I have to get to Oraibi."

"Oh, well I live just down the street," he said. "You wanna hang out there?"

Martin caught on and jumped in. "Hey Arlen. I'm gonna take off. I'll drop you off at your place on my way by." Martin looked at me as I shuffled around. "You stay here. I'm just going to visit a friend of mine, and then I'll be right back."

He led his kids and Arlen out to the truck and took off.

A few minutes of silence passed and I noticed a familiar plant I enjoy smoking. Walter and I talked about the herb for a bit before Martin returned.

"You know, Arlen was going to rob you right?" He came in saying to me.

"Yeah?" I played the fool.

"Yeah, that's why he was asking about your stuff. He was waiting to get you alone, beat you up and take your money," he said. "You've gotta watch out up here. They'll come knocking on your door in the middle of the night, 'hey man, open up. We're brothers right?' Then you open the door, they jump your ass and steal your shit. It's like that up here, man." He cracked open a beer, chugged it immediately, crushed the can in his hand and threw it on the floor.

"One time, I had to kill my cousin right outside here. He got too rowdy one night, threatened me and brought on a fight. He tried to kill me, so I killed him first. You can't let anybody get the advantage, man. If they come at you with a knife, it doesn't matter where they stab you, you have to stop it. Block it with your hand, let them stab right through it; it'll hurt like hell, but get that knife away from them and kill them. That's what you gotta do."

The whole time he's talking about this, I'm digging through my bag looking for the pair of scissors and the pepper spray I brought. He noticed the pepper spray when I took it out.

"That shit doesn't work. You spray 'em in the face, they just keep coming," he informed. "You gotta stab em, or shoot em, otherwise they'll kill you."

Then Walter chimed in, "Why'd you come here?"

"I have a plan to take back Turtle Island," I said with confidence. I knew about the legends of the Lost White Brother. I was white, a brother to all and certainly lost.

Walter stared at me for a moment before closing his eyes. "We've been waiting for you."

"Well, I don't believe in none of that religious bullshit. God, religion, none of it, just a bunch of brainwashing crap," Martin defended. "This place is no good, full of shit."

I stayed silent and let him continue his rant. By the end, I knew that this was no place for me. It was far from safe for a lonely traveler. When Martin was leaving, he asked where I planned to go. I asked if he could take me back to the cultural center. He was already going that way.

Martin was a reckless and fast driver. Eight beers in, two kids without seat belts and no law enforcement in the wild west could stop him from speeding across the plains. I was nervous the whole ride, but we never crashed. We arrived back at the cultural center and I opened the door. I gave his kids two lucky coins and said my thanks.

The cultural center was welcoming now, familiar. I stayed there and planned for tomorrow again.

The next day came and I had no money.

"We don't take debit cards," said the clerk, "Cash or credit only."

"Is there an ATM?" I asked.

"Yeah, at the store in Kyokotsville."

"Oh. Damn. Thanks." I had already walked to this store yesterday, and I was forced there again. I had left later in the day and the sunlight was fading faster. I knew I wouldn't make it back before nightfall, but it was better than walking around in the sun. I used the ATM for some cash and headed back.

I turned around at the Oraibi wash and looked back to where I was supposed to be. The sun was setting and the mesa had rays of light beaming out from behind it. It was beautiful.

Next time. I was too afraid.

I spent the night outside to save myself some money, assurance I could return home. Two bright stars, one on top of the other, watched me from above. In the distance, clouds periodically sparked with electric light. Two dogs stayed close and kept guard all night. I set the alarm on my phone to wake me up when it turned bright.

The next morning, I caught the bus and headed home - empty handed, all alone.

Greyhound

I left the reservation and couldn't wait to head home. I returned to the motel to retrieve Epi and my other bag. The motel owner was kind and gave me a ride to the bus station in his truck.

It didn't take long to buy a ticket and process my bags. I was glad to have a direction after being so aimless, even if it was backwards.

While I was there, I met a homeless traveler named Boxcar in the parking lot. He was a military preacher who knew Hebrew and enjoyed the Bible. We walked around town talking about politics, waiting for our departure time. He told me the story of how a fellow train-jumping vagrant gave him the nickname Boxcar. He was trying to make his way back home to Florida. His wife ditched him in a Las Vegas casino, after stealing eighteen thousand dollars of his winnings. Then she drove away in his Cadillac. It was hilariously unfortunate and all he could do was laugh about it now.

~~~

"I don't know my name, but it begins with an A," I admitted.

He thought for a moment, "Admiral. That's your name." Carrying on the tradition.

"*Admiral*, I like it. I am the captain of this vessel!"

He took me to a local shelter where I could clean up and shower. We talked about religion for most of the time. I bought him a forty and we shared a box of smokes. Drinking in public was illegal, but we both had an extra sense. The ring in our ears came simultaneously; a warning.

"We've gotta go," he said.
~~~

“Yep,” I knew. I heard it too.

We started walking down the street. A police car drove by us. We watched as the patrol car turned around at the spot where we had been sitting. We turned the corner out of sight. A moment later, the car turned the corner after us. The officer stopped, got out and ran our records. The computer revealed that Boxcar had a warrant. The officer had to arrest him.

“The Lord's got a mission for me elsewhere. Take care of yourself and may God bless,” he said to me.

We hugged and said goodbye. He missed his bus.

That was the third homeless guy who had blessed me that day.

~~~

“It's like a movie,” I said. The group I traveled with finally got comfortable in their seats.

This was my second day on the bus. We all met waiting at the Dallas station for eight hours. The crew was: a beautiful Yaqui Indian woman named Carmen traveling with her teenage daughter, two traveling lesbians, a righteous white-gangster nicknamed Smokey, and myself – the Admiral. It was a match made in heaven.

We spent a few days together, enjoying our trip and our humors. I danced in cowboy boots to the peanut butter-jelly song for Carmen and her camera phone at one of our stops. They asked me to do it a few more times as the trip went on, but the first one had the real magic of spontaneity.

At one stop an attractive brown woman walked on the bus. Smokey immediately started talking to her.

“Hey. You're pretty, girl. What's your name?” She smiled and answered. I had the only open seat and she asked to sit next to me. I stood up to let her in.
~~~

"You see how fast he got up when you asked to sit down?" He joked, laughter exploded across the bus. "He blushin' now. He must really like you," Smokey continued. "Yeah, his cheeks is beat red." Everybody within earshot was laughing. It was hilarious, but I wasn't interested in meeting girls on this trip.

We lost the lesbian couple at Tennessee. Carmen and her daughter departed at Nashville, and Smokey and I rode together until New York. He told me stories of how he'd been shot twice and showed me the scars. They weren't fatal wounds, but the stories were scary enough.

Smokey and I had the same birthday and the upcoming weekend was our weekend. We exchanged numbers to congratulate each other, but I never resurrected my phone to do so.

~~~

Broke and demoralized, I arrived at the closest bus station to my house. Charlie picked me up. When I returned home, I saw a new addition next to my bedroom door. It was the picture my Dad had been framing of the spaceship and cowboy.

Charlie and I spent the night together and talked. She was surprised at how soon I had returned. I was only gone for a couple of weeks, but she was glad I was back and safe. I told her how uneventful it was out west and we smoked some herb to celebrate.

The conversation hit a patch of silence. She picked up a book laying on my end table, flipped open to a random page, and read a piece of it out loud: "Maybe there was a purpose to it? Maybe I was supposed to come back empty handed?"

My thoughts stopped dead in their tracks. *What?* All
~~~

logical filters went out the window. *Was that about me?*

Charlie smiled, closed the book and returned it to the end table.

How? I failed. I was too stunned to speak.

Why Dream?

I, to this day, continue to wake up and wish for world peace and harmony. I know it's possible because I have a genie in me. When I walked through the world, it was peaceful and I seemed safe even when I knew I wasn't. However, it's the harmony we all lack. We all know how to play our piece, but we don't know how to play them together.

I want to design a government that will generate peace. There will be no bombs or weapons of mass destruction, or conflicts over money and wars. Money will be wise, food will be abundant, and we'll share it with everyone so no one will need it.

I want to design a nation to encourage the pursuit of dreams. One with unlimited employment, unlimited potential and the access to the knowledge that will get us there; where teachers receive the compensation they deserve and students receive the expenses they compensate for.

I want to design an environment that will promote nature to live with us, just as much as we live within it: an ecosystem of color and smells, where nature has an equal right to prosper; a biosphere of empathy for the awareness of our environment, which is also aware of us. There's an unheard of amount of jobs cleaning the trash from this world.

I want to design a social system independent from money; a class average where no one goes hungry or sick without care; a scientific adventure to encourage the intellect, and sustainable means to achieve the highest common standard of living; a plan on which to grow with nature, not alone.

I want to design my home.

In my bedroom, I bent down on one knee. I closed my eyes and prayed to the Universe.

Hello. Is there any way for world peace and harmony?

A loud, deep hum burst into my head. My eyes forced themselves open.

It heard me.

Entanglement

I leaped off the floor to my feet and looked up in absolute shock and horror. The bedroom door opened and disappeared. My once carpeted floor transformed into warm, dry grass that crushed under my shoes. The walls disappeared and revealed a view distant and vast, blanketed with electricity and light behind it. It was once midnight, but the moon was just rising. The air switched from stale smoke to a fresh, clean breeze carrying a salty hint of the ocean.

I was on top of a hill. The view was beautiful. A golden pyramid illuminated above the other structures in the distance. I couldn't begin to recognize where I was, but I felt strangely familiar with it.

I padded myself with my hands. My clothes were still on. I wore blue jeans and a white slim-fit collared dress shirt, no tie. Brown loafers covered my feet. I dressed to impress. Here, it was not cold at all.

Where am I? This is beautiful.

I turned around to a building housing a giant bucket on top and wondered in awe.

What is this place for?

I made my way towards the strange house.

It looks like a funnel.

I knocked on the door. It was silent. I knocked again. There was some rustling on the other side. Excited, I watched the knob spin. I had no idea what was opening to me.

"Hello. What may I do for you?" A young woman greeted me. I couldn't believe her beauty. She was short with long, brown hair and a youthful, round face. A lavender dress hugged the length of her body. The ripples in the velvet silk shined around her curves. She was divine.

"Hi, umm, nice to meet you," I uttered, nervously brushing my eyebrow. "My name is Alef." Her almond eyes smiled with innocence. My heart jumped into my throat. "Who are you?" I choked.

"Jeen. It's nice to meet you, too." We stared into each other for a moment. Her hazel eyes teased the appetite to my soul.

"What's the funnel on top for?" I asked, just trying to think of something to say. She turned bewildered for a moment.

"You don't know?" She asked slowly, still looking confused.

I shrugged.

She motioned with her hand. *Never mind.* "It helps clean the cities underground waste management system. This funnel collects rain water and once a year the four corners flush at the same time. It's quite a celebrated event."

I laughed, "That's funny. Is that why you're here?"

"Yeah..." Her voice trailed off. "Why are you here?" She looked frightened.

"I don't know, just got -." She cut me off.

"From where?"

"My room," I answered.

There was a pause as she wondered.

"Who are you Alef?" Her voice was stern.

"What?"

"What?" She mocked in anger. "Who are you Alef?"

"I don't understand what you're asking!"

"Tell me who you are, now!"

"Alef! My name is Alef!" I shouted.

"What are you doing here?" She yelled

"I don't know!"

"Then leave." With that, she slammed the door.

"Sorry!" I yelled back through the door stunned. "I don't know where I am!"

There was silence on the other side. I turned around and started walking towards the city. The lights looked so far away, but I was eager to explore them. Behind me I heard the door to the funnel house quickly swing back open. The light from inside jumped out towards me. I turned around.

"Just kidding!" She yelled, laughing. "It's you!"

"What?" I asked, confused and stunned. The light from inside outlined her silhouette. The dark figure was as beautiful as when she was in color.

"It's you!" She repeated, coming towards me.

"Who am I?" Sarcasm. *This woman is insane.*

"You're the King!" I could hear the excitement in her voice.

"What? Where?" I asked, scratching my head, slightly worried.

"I know! Funny, right?" She smiled, taking advantage of my confusion.

We were face to face again.

"What?" I asked.

"That you don't know where you are. It's funny."

"What?"

"What?" She mocked, moving her neck back and forth in coy exaggeration. It was so silly looking that my smile broke the fog of confusion.

"Where am I?"

"You built this place," she said. A look of horror crossed my face. *This woman is insane.*

She laughed. "Come in. I'll tell you."

"Okay," I passively agreed.

Funnel Hut

Jeen led me into the building. The front room was open and wide besides the gigantic silver funnel descending from the ceiling and leading down into the floor. There was a door on every wall, but only one had light sneaking out from the crack underneath. She led me through the door into a bright dining room with a big, round table surrounded by chairs. The thick scent of a stew flooded the air. The room was bland, white, with a fridge and microwave for food - no stove. Only a clock and calendar adorned the wall. It was the standard employee cafeteria.

There was a smorgasbord of fruits and vegetables waiting on the table. She motioned for me to sit as she moved towards a cart in the back of the room. She knelt down and opened a door on the cart.

"Want anything hot to eat or drink?" Jeen asked.

"Oh, no thanks," I was hungry, but not for food. She pulled a container from the cart and emptied it into the stew.

"So, where am I?"

"You're in Avalon – the greatest nation ever made." She looked up at me and smiled quickly before returning to her stew.

"Wow!" I laughed in disbelief. "Like King Arthur?"

"Who?"

"King Arthur, you know, the boy King of England." She stared at me, blankly. "He pulled the legendary sword Excalibur from the stone," I continued, but she knew nothing.

"England hasn't existed for," she paused, calculating. "Probably a hundred years."

"What?" My heart jumped.

"Yeah, Most of the world is gone now. One of the

nation’s saw its own end coming and went berserk, just blew up everything. The poverty got so bad in America that we couldn't stay and support everyone anymore and departed. Oh! Avalon floats, if you didn't know that. So, we don't know what they do on land anymore.”

“Wow.” I paused in silence, but went frantic in my head. “Saw that one coming,” I laughed the anxiety off. “I don't know what else to say. This place is beautiful.” I looked at her.

“Yeah.” Her eyes trailed off. She looked sad for a moment.

“So, why are you here?”

“The flush is tonight.” She stared at the table.

“To clean the waste?” I asked. She nodded. “When?”

“Midnight.”

“When is that?”

“Three hours from now.”

“Oh.” I paused. “Why are you sad?” She looked up at me, then back down at the table.

“I'm going alone.”

“That's okay. So am I. We can be alone, together!” I threw my fist into the air, like I was starting a revolution. She looked up and smiled.

“You don't understand. It's already like that,” she paused. “We're still together, but he's left me for someone better. He doesn't think I know, but I found out.” Jeen was right. She was together, alone.

“That's not good,” I said, inhaling deeply. “There are better women than you here?” I don't believe it,” I joked innocently. She smiled at the compliment.

“Yeah, it's okay though,” she lied.

“Yeah, He's a bag of dicks,” I said. She quickly glanced at me.

"Lots of them," I reinforced, holding her gaze and smiling. She giggled. A moment of silence passed. Jeen broke it.

"Quite a special night for you."

"Why?"

"This food is for the Architects," she said.

"Who are the Architects?"

"They're the ones who built Avalon after you made it."

"I didn't make this."

"You will." She said it so nonchalant.

"How?"

"I don't know, but you figured it out."

"Figured what out?"

"I don't really know," she laughed. "I'm not a history buff, but I do know that no one has ever died by starvation here. My teachers said it was never like this on land."

"Wow. Nope. Certainly not. There's a whole continent full of starving people and the fat people won't feed them. We just don't understand." I paused. "Hey. This may seem like an odd question, but what year is it?"

"2112," she answered. I was far away from home in distance *and* time.

"Today's Tom Sawyer..." I laughed to myself.

"What?"

"Just a song." The nostalgia made me feel comfortable. "So, when are the Architects showing up?"

"About another hour or so, they'll be excited to meet you."

"Why?" I laughed.

"They never got to meet you." She slipped. Her face turned serious and she paused and stared at the table, waiting for my curiosity.

"Uhh... why?" I asked again.

"You were already dead," she said, quietly, with her head down.

"Well, sorry for asking!" I joked. She smiled.

I stared at the table for a long moment as the truth sank in.

"How?" I had to ask. "How did I die?" I couldn't help it.

"Somebody shot you."

"Oh." *Typical.*

"Yeah, I remember learning about it in grade school. You declared war," she paused and smiled to herself. "You declared war on war."

I laughed. "Yeah, that sounds like me."

There was another silence.

"Did we win?" I asked.

"Yes." She laughed.

We did.

The Architects

Jeen and I talked until there was a knock on the door.

"I wonder who's first," Jeen said as she stood up to answer it.

Butterflies flew into my stomach when she left the room. *Am I dreaming?*

I heard Jeen open the door and a loud male voice boomed into the building.

"Hiya Jeeny! How are ya?" I could hear his boots enter the building almost as loud as his voice.

"Awesome! Yourself?" She quickly replied.

"Excited!" He boomed. "You are too excited. What for? Put some extra spice in my stew this year?" He was a quick talker and his boots were getting closer.

I could hear Jeeny giggle at him as she led the boots into the room. We made eye contact.

"Holy shit! It's you!" He yelled. He was not as tall as his voice. "Awesome!" He laughed out loud.

"Yeah, I thought it was pretty cool." I replied.

He laughed even louder. I stood up as he made his way over to shake my hand. He was an older man, probably in his fifties and wore a long, brown coat that buttoned up over a white undershirt. A gold pocket square shined in his left chest pocket below a rainbow pin. The pin had seven sides. I looked closer. It was a heptagon pointing to the heavens.

"My name is Ayen, and I already know you," he said as we shook hands. His blue jeans and loafers contrasted his professional look.

"Yeah, that seems to be the trend."

He laughed. We both sat at the table as Jeeny poured Ayen a bowl of stew.

"How'd you get here?" He asked.

"I don't know. Am I dreaming?" It made him laugh.

"Boy, aren't we all," he said, philosophically. Jeeny brought his stew over.

"See?" He looked at me, then at her as she set the bowl down on the table. "Thanks for making my dreams come true, girl."

Her almond eyes smiled a familiar innocence.

"You're welcome, boy."

"Oh, no, you did not just call me a boy, miss." He replied smiling, teeth drawn, encouraging the argument.

"You know, I am no little girl. I am old enough to do what I please," Jeeny teased back.

Damn, she is good. I thought to myself.

"Fine," he surrendered. "You can win this time."

"Just like last time," she said, smiling in victory.

"Meh," Ayen grumbled, then smiled.

We all laughed.

Ayen pulled the bowl of stew up to his nose and let out a long, deep moan.

"You're such a weirdo," Jeeny said, turning back to the food cart.

"It's all your fault," he flirted back, looking at her. Then he looked at me, pointing towards her with his thumb. "Jeeny is a wizard with vegetables, she's turnin' me into one." I could hear her laughing.

Ayen looked up behind me at the clock on the wall.

"So, right," Ayen boomed raising his spoon in the air to revolt. "Let's get down to business, shall we? I... am the Master Chief Architect here." He paused and lowered the spoon, pointing it at me, "and we've got to friggin' hide you."

"Okay," I giggled.

He dumped his spoon in the stew and quickly drew

it to his mouth.

"Ah. Bliss," he said, setting his spoon back in the stew. He looked at Jeeny. "Keep this warm for me, my dear! We will be right back!" He declared like a king.

We stood up and he led me out of the room. There was a knock on the door.

"Quick," he whispered, leading me around the funnel and opening a door on the other side.

"Stay in here. I'll be back in, like, ten minutes tops."

"Okay."

~~~

So, there I was. In a dark room in the catch basin of a poop shooting waste management system. This room had a brown desk with a computer on it. A calendar hung on the wall behind the desk. I took a seat in the computer chair. The machine wasn't on. I closed my eyes and waited.

I could hear the front door opening from where I was hiding. Many voices greeted Jeeny and Ayen's laughter boomed over them all.

She is so sweet, I thought to myself. All of the Architects seemed to know her. There was silence for a few minutes and then the door flew open. I opened my eyes.

Ayen walked in. "Ready for your close up?"

"No," I smiled.

"Good."

He led me back around the funnel into the room full of Architects.

"Guess what fell from the sky?" He declared as we walked into the room.

There was a silent pause as everyone connected the dots, followed by laughter and cheering.

"Thanks. I flew in on a stork," I joked. They
~~~

laughed again and stood up to shake my hand. It was weird being praised for the future. After all the greeting commotion, they made their way back to the table.

"Sit and have a meal with us," Ayen invited. "I'm sure we all have lots of questions."

"Cool. Thanks, but I've only got one question," I paused. "Am I dead?"

The room burst into laughter and they all raised their glasses.

"No one dies in paradise!"

Paradise

There were eleven Architects in total and they were very enthusiastic about Avalon. They said it was the first prototype of a series of floating cities to promote sustainable population growth.

"Avalon was the only Paradise Prototype made," said the oldest man in the room. Earlier, when we shook hands, he had introduced himself as Odey. He continued, "my father used to work for the government before the system imploded. Once the world had proof it could work, it reacted like a cancer. Governments toppled and cities started burning up in zealous envy of change. Robberies happened daily and, if you were wearing a business suit, you were likely slaughtered in the street. It was absolute chaos. No one could have predicted it. We've departed from land twice. Once, during the world riots and the last time after the global depression. Then-"

"Stop with all the sad shit, Ode," Ayen interrupted. "Basically, the world didn't know how to handle a society that was just too awesome and, like a moth to a flame, we flew head first into the fire. Avalon intended to safely depopulate areas to rebuild them with more sustainable design, but no..."

"This is a fully functioning self-sustainable city," interrupted Ode. "Have you been into it yet?"

"No." I replied, looking down.

"Oh. Well, Ayen will have to take you on a tour before he bores you to death explaining about it," Ode jokingly attacked, "but, basically, there's enough clean water and food growing everywhere, there's way too many houses than there are people and we are all very well-educated." He raised his glass. "All we need."

"We are free to explore our interests and dreams,"

chimed in Marjorie, a middle-aged woman.

"There are no worries here," said another Architect named Keith.

"And barely any crime, besides the occasional psychopath," corrected Ayen. "It doesn't go without fault though, the politicians are still retarded." We all laughed.

"You couldn't fix that," said Ode. They all laughed again.

"I, honestly, have no idea what I did."

"That's why you're here," said a young man who had introduced himself as Zane. "We aren't really architects, as in builders, per say." He smiled.

"We're architects of reality," concluded Ayen. "We never knew how you figured it out, how you put this world together, if not had you actually been here. So, we waited until this day you would bend the world and meet us." The room went silent for a moment in agreement. *Today was that day.*

"Bend the world?" I asked.

"We call it the God spot," said Ayen. "It can happen to all of us, usually as deja vu, but it's rare in this capacity."

"You created a whole nation from a dream practical enough to build," Zane praised. "Then we built it."

"Out of trash!" Keith yelled. They all laughed.

"Avalon is your dream come true," said Ode. "For all of us."

"We all remember our dreams can come true." Zane looked at me, "because of you."

The room went silent. A weird sadness hung over it.

"We're all screwed," Ayen joked.

The room laughed. I chuckled too, but it wasn't comforting.

The Flush

It was still a half hour until the flush. The Architects had dispersed to the other three corners of Avalon, waiting to pull the levers. Jeeny, Ayen, Ode and I basked in the silence for a moment.

After a minute passed, Ayen took a deep breath.

"Right! That was nice. Let's get down to business, shall we?" He looked at me. "You... have to learn what you did, really fast. I've got a bad feeling about this."

"Okay," I nodded.

"First, Avalon floats on a ballast system made from, what was, but no longer is, garbage island," Ayen said.

"Garbage island?"

"Yeah, it was a massive vortex of plastic in the Pacific Ocean. You urged the people to clean it up and recycle it into an island for the future. Due to the fear of over population, Avalon was the first of many planned renewable cities."

"That never got built, like Atlantis." Ode interrupted. "That paradise could have been three times the size of Avalon."

"Yes," agreed Ayen. "After the world riots, survival became top priority – nobody wanted to build paradise anymore. To us, survival isn't a hassle. That's what Avalon was for. This society has enough food to sustain well over twice its current population."

"And we haven't begun to reach a challenging population size, yet," Ode joined in. "After the global depression, we fed half of America. Granted, America was vastly depopulated by then"

"The global depression?" I asked.

"Yeah, the world tried to turn around too fast and they broke their necks," Ayen laughed. I didn't understand the metaphor.

"The world was in terrible financial shape," Ode said. "A fiscal crisis in many nations – even the top super powers of their time had many monetary mishaps with each other, until you."

"You saw the devil behind it all and eliminated the need for money," Ayen said. "Those who loved money tried hard to fight it and keep its value, slandering you and Avalon with irrational fears."

"We don't know who fired first," Ode said, "but when you died, everyone went crazy."

"Why?" I asked. There was silence.

"You were right and we all knew it," Ode said. "You brought the truth and hope and when that faded..."

"They tried to turn around too fast," Ayen repeated, "and they all broke their necks." Now, I knew what it meant. There was a long pause. Ayen looked at me with squinted eyes.

"No pressure," he said. We all laughed. "I'll make a lesson plan for tomorrow."

"Yeah, come by the lodge after noon and we'll teach you the rest about Avalon," Ode said. "Have you made friends with Jeeny?"

"Yeah," Jeeny jumped in before I could answer. "I'll take him in tonight." She looked at me and smiled.

"Thank you." I returned the smile and nodded.

"Right! You buncha queers," Ayen declared. "Let's get this shit show started shall we? How much time is left?"

"Fifteen minutes," Ode replied.

"Damn. I don't want to wait anymore. How'd you jump here, God spotter?" Ayen asked, looking at me.

"Jump?" I repeated.

"Yeah, quantum entanglement," Ayen answered. "You know, when two things happen at two different places in two different times at the same time."

"Two things? Two different? What?" We all laughed.

"Yeah. You are Here, but you came from There; from the past, to the future," Ayes said. "How'd you do it?"

"Oh, I made a wish."

"A wish?" Ayen's tone grew serious. "To whom?"

"The Universe," I answered.

"Hmm," Ayen pondered a moment. "Something's missing."

"Your heart," Ode jumped in.

"Pfft, I have a heart," Ayen argued. "It just sat outside too long and now it's covered in lust." We laughed. There was a long silence after.

Ode pointed to the both of us.

"You two should go downtown tonight and celebrate," he said. "I'll clean the cart out."

"And I'll help!" Ayen stood up, excited.

"Thanks," answered Jeeny. "I'll be back to pick it up tomorrow."

"It'll be here," said Ode.

"And empty," said Ayen, opening the pot of stew with a big grin. We laughed. Jeeny motioned to me.

"You ready?" She asked, standing up.

"Yep," I lied, mirroring her.

I shook hands with the two Architects and said goodbye.

"You kiddos have a good night," Ayen said with a wink.

I looked down at the floor. Ayen laughed when he saw my fear. I followed Jeeny out of the room.

"The courageous only leaps and bounds for dreams!" Ayen yelled as we opened the door to the outside.

~~~

"Over here," Jeeny said as she led me down a cement walkway around the left of the building. It was dark now, but small, dim lights in the ground illuminated the path. She led me to a door and opened it. Behind it was a stairway and she proceeded down it. I followed.

"What is this?" I asked.

"The rail."

"There's a train here?"

"Yeah. It's the fastest way to travel."

"What about cars?" I asked.

"We have cars. There isn't much need of them though," she said, "but they turbo 'em up and race 'em anyway."

"You still use gas?"

"No," Jeeny laughed. "We use bio-diesel from plant oils for racing. Most of the cars are electric. They charge themselves."

"Cool," I said. "When does the train come?"

"It's already here, just have to notify it." At the bottom of the stairs was a familiar pair of silver reflective doors. She pressed a button on the wall. Sounds of movement echoed behind the door.

"Is this an elevator?"

"No," she laughed, "well, yeah, but it goes sideways."

"Oh, a horizontalator." I nodded scientifically. She giggled.

A moment later the doors opened up and we entered the box.

"Ready?"

"Sure."

She pressed a button and a burst of air shot out from
~~~

under the box. The door closed and there was silence.

"Hold on."

I grabbed the side-rail, but the force pushed me off-balance and I stumbled around on my feet like a drunkard desperately searching for equilibrium.

"Whoa!" I yelled. "This is great."

"Yeah," she agreed, "and really fast."

Five minutes passed and the rail stopped. The door to the box opened revealing a platform of people waiting to get into their own personal boxes.

"What is this?"

"This is the central hub. All the rails transport here. They go everywhere and anywhere you want them too, but," she paused. "Keep your head down," she said, grabbing my hand. I looked at the floor as she quickly led me past a crowd of waiting people. She let go when we reached a staircase.

The stairs led up into extraordinary noise. The closer we reached the top of the stairs, the louder it became. When we reached the top, the city was alive with music, lights and people. Colors flooded the cones in my eyes from the bright trees and flowers that adorned the futuristic scene. It was like the Star Trek Enterprise had crashed into the garden of Eden.

People flooded the streets. A little girl breached the top of the crowd to pick a vibrant red apple from a nearby tree. Some were picking berries and putting them into baskets while others walked by in business suits talking into a phone, blindly familiar of the beauty. The white noise of chatter drowned the air. A monorail screeched to a halt in the distance.

"Welcome to Camelot - the center of paradise."

Inner Circle

The street was extraordinarily wide and crowded. People were walking about everywhere. There were no cars, but the road divided with the familiar solid yellow double lines. I looked around. Bicycle paths cut out around the sides of the street for their own designated routes, but the streets were too crowded to allow it. I looked up. The night sky reflected off of the buildings, mirroring the heavens.

"It looks like it stretches all the way up into space," I said.

"The buildings are covered in sun catching cells," she replied.

"Wow!" I yelled as we ventured further. "This is huge!"

"Yes, Camelot is probably two hundred meters high," Jeeny said, looking around. She took my hand, "This way."

She led me into the crowd, across the street. We crossed to the sidewalk of a large white building. I looked around. All the buildings reached to the ceiling. Grapes and other vines hung down from their lowest ledges. We were inside the base level of a gigantic social mall.

"All business, education, governance, etc. It all takes place here in one of these buildings. We live on the second ring."

"The second ring?" I asked, as she led me blindly down the sidewalk. "How many rings are there?"

"Three," she answered. "The center is where we are, the second is where we live and the outer ring is where our food and fuel come from."

"Wow," I said, amazed. "How big?"

"Oh," she paused in thought, "around twenty-seven

square miles total."

"Cool. How many people?"

"Well over a million so far," she said, walking again.

"And where are we going?" I finally asked. *Jeesh. I'm annoying.*

"To the party!" She looked back with a smile.

"Right on!"

~~~

My eyes wandered like a child at a carnival. There were no gray areas. The buildings were shaped, painted and geometrically exquisite. Triangles squared off and spiraled the walls in circles. The whole city was a mathematical canvas.

We walked for another minute or so before we reached the center square. I stood next to her looking at a giant cinema on all sides. A suited man was giving a speech to the crowd. A countdown descended in the corner of the screen. *47 seconds.*

"Just in time," Jeeny yelled. "Woo!"

"Who's that man?"

"That's the President," she laughed and grabbed my hand. *40 seconds.*

"Hey! You!" A man's voice boomed in our direction from afar. Jeeny quickly released my hand. I knew who it was and he was angry. I turned my head toward the voice.

"Who the fuck are you?" The voice cut through the air again. He was a giant man, dressed well in a black suit and tie. I looked down at his fists clenching as he approached.

"You're dead!" He yelled, pointing directly at me. I
~~~

raised my eyebrows in surprise. He wasn't stopping. I stepped towards him, into stance and looked back at his face, waiting for it.

His upper lip curled and his teeth drew. *There.* His right arm looped out. I darted under it and spun around, slamming my fist like a hammer into the side of his chin. He dropped to the ground.

"Run!" I yelled at Jeeny. She watched frozen, emotionless.

"Run!" I yelled again, grabbing her hand. She snapped to and quickly followed me away from the scene. I looked back. The giant was starting to stand, looking around for us. We sliced through the crowd away from him.

"Sorry! Sorry!" I could hear Jeeny yelling from behind. I looked at the next screen. *27 seconds.*

We ran to the screen opposite to the one we entered, and stopped. I looked up at the countdown. *15 seconds.*

"Sorry!" She apologized again, mid breath. Jeeny was hysterical. "I didn't know he would-"

"That was awesome!" I yelled, cutting her off. "I'm sorry for enjoying it!"

The screen switched to show the crowd. They started counting down. *10!* The crowd cheered.

9*!* Jeeny gave me a confused smile.

8*!* She moved closer to me.

7*!* I took her other hand.

6*!* We stared into each other. The crowd roared louder.

5*!* Her almond eyes gleamed a familiar innocence.

4*!* She looked down at my lips.

3*!* I motioned my face close to hers. She waited.

2*!* I paused looking into her. I could feel her breath.

1! We closed our eyes.

Woo! She pressed her face into mine.

The crowd exploded as we kissed. Her soft lips danced with mine as my heart fluttered faster than the wings of a hummingbird. We both pulled away, smiling. My heart melted in my chest. She wrapped her arms around me for another embrace. I could feel the exhale from her nose on my upper lip. *This was paradise.*

~~~

A loud crack ruptured through the air. The ground violently lunged up and quickly receded again. Then silence. Jeeny grabbed me tight. The screen went black.

"This isn't right," she said, tightening her hold.

The crowd remained quiet in silent horror. A minute passed before the screen switched back to the President.

"Hello, proud citizens of Avalon. This is a disaster level event," he said calmly. "Our monitors are showing that a pipe ruptured in the third corner causing sufficient underground damage. The rupture," he paused, blinking wildly. "The rupture forced multiple ballast supports into the sea. At this moment in time," he paused again, tears filling his eyes, "Avalon is sinking."
~~~

Capsized

The President's voice boomed their worst fears.

"We're trying the best we can to remedy the situation and steer ourselves towards land," he figured, "but even if we fix this, we don't know how long it will hold. Reaching land is our greatest priority. Please proceed to the loading docks and plan for evacuation. I love you and may God bless us all."

The screen switched to blue and there was silence. Then, an automated message boomed throughout the city: "Please, proceed to the loading docks for evacuation. Kindly proceed to the loading docks for evacuation."

Paradise was sinking. The crowd exploded in horror and started to scatter in a feared stampede. Shrieks and screams pierced the crowd as people fell to the ground as other screams shoved through to help them up.

Jeeny and I stood still and watched in shock as the horror played out.

"You have to go to the lodge!" Jeeny yelled through the noise.

"Where's that?!"

"I'll take you!" She looked around frantically. "Quick!"

She grabbed my hand and led me across the plaza, towards the way we came in from.

"Hey!" I heard a voice yell towards me, but I paid no attention. We kept running, making our way across the plaza. Jeeny stopped, took a deep breath, and reached into her pocket. She pulled out a slim piece of plastic and shook it. It flashed on. She fumbled around with her fingers on the screen before putting it to her ear. She grabbed my hand and we continued to run.

"I need the grand lodge please," she said. A moment

went by. “I'm bringing him there.” We turned a corner.

“Okay,” she said into the device.

“Hey!” The voice boomed into my ear. Gravity shifted and I smashed to the ground. The giant held me in place by my neck as I tried to squirm away. Helpless, I looked up at Jeeny. I heard a scream as the man's fist eclipsed my view.

~~~

“Hey.” A soft voice broke through the darkness.

“Hey.” It repeated. I opened my eyes. The wrinkled face of an older man was crouched in front of me.

“Hey, are you okay?” He asked as he stood up.

“Yeah, I think so,” I said. The right side of my face ached and there was blood smeared under my nose. I looked around. Jeeny was gone.

The old man helped me up.

“Thank you sir,” I said to him.

“I saw the beating you took,” he said, “nasty man.”

“Yeah,” I replied, “great girl though.” The old man laughed.

“I recognize you from somewhere,” he said, pausing, “but I don't remember where. What's your name?” He asked.

“Alef,” I said.

“That's a familiar name,” he replied. “Great name from a great man.” He paused. “My name is Gev.”

“Nice to meet you, Gev,” I said as we shook hands.

“Do you know where the grand lodge is?” I asked him.

He thought for a moment.

“Yes,” he said slowly. “I'll take you there. Umm,” he paused, thinking, “This way.”
~~~

He led me out of the center square and down a street. The buildings rose to the heavens on the sides. He led me across towards another open square. The crowd was scattering as they made their way toward the loading shores.

"This was the first square ever built here," the old man commented, pointing to a small park as we walked by. A bronzed statue of a man playing a guitar watched over the square.

"I remember it from when I was a kid, this park," he said, as he stopped and looked at me. A loud boom rumbled through the air. Gev and I hit the ground as it bubbled up and tore the park apart. The grass ripped from the earth and chunks of dirt carried objects into the sky. Sand rained on us as I tried to look around. A loud metal clang cracked through the noise. A moment later, another clang ruptured the air. It was getting closer.

Vvvt!

An object smashed into the side of a car directly behind us. Glass exploded onto us as the front end of the car folded around it. Broken shards of metal separated and crashed to the ground. The ground stopped rumbling and everything went silent.

"Hey!" Gev yelled out, the dirt finally ending its downpour. "You okay?"

"Yes!" I yelled back, looking around. My ears were ringing. We collected ourselves for a moment. I stood up first and helped the old man to his feet.

"The statue is gone," I said, pointing to it down the street. I looked over into the car behind us. A long nose protruded from the wreckage. I couldn't believe what I was seeing. Gev saw it too.

"It's you!" He yelled. "I thought so!" He pulled me in fast and hugged me.

"You're here! To save us!" He yelled, looking to the sky in excited praise.

"I'm afraid I can't save you," I said looking at the ground in disappointment. "I don't even know how I got here or how I made this."

He went silent for a moment and looked at me.

"That's okay," he said, shrugging it off. "We'll get you to the grand lodge and you'll figure this all out."

He turned around and, with a march of purpose, continued leading me through the streets.

~~~

"It's that temple over there," Gev said as he pointed across an intersection. The light post had fallen down and colored glass spread out across the street

"They'll want to see you!" He laughed.

"Thanks for all your help," I said, shaking his hand.

"No. Thank you," he said, "for doing this. I had a great life here."

I nodded. I didn't know what to say.

"Good luck," he said as he turned to walk away.

"Godspeed!" I yelled after him. I turned around.

"You were older in the statue!" Gev yelled back through the distance.

The temple was beautiful from the outside, adorned with guardian angels, flowers and blooming vines. Golden delicious apples dangled across the front yard fenced in by tall, green hedges. Cracks rippled and broke through the street, but there was no damage on the temple grounds. The grass looked perfect.

I started to cross the street. The temple door swung open and Ayen came bursting out. He stopped when he saw
~~~

me.

"Hurry! Get into the temple!" He yelled, beckoning me over with his hand. "Hurry! We've got to teach you!"

I ran up the stairs. The front walls displayed beautiful colored shapes and geometric symbols with enlarged words like peace and love. Ayen held the door open as I entered.

"Where's Jeeny?" I asked, darting into a small carpeted room.

"I don't know," Ayen replied. "What happened to your head?"

"Boyfriend," I said quickly. Ayen gave me a confused look, then laughed out loud.

"Jeeny's dangerous!" He joked.

"Where is she?" I quickly asked.

"I don't know," Ayen said.

"So, what do we do, now?" I was frantic.

"Well," Ayen paused to think. "The people here are staying and... we are leaving."

"What does that mean?" I asked.

"You'll see us in history, my friend," Ayen said. "Just like you, we'll already be dead, but you'll know about us and we'll carry this nation through history."

"In history?"

"Yes, we're going back in time," Ayen said. "You came forward to take us back with you. This is just a-"

The ground shook and the building rippled back and forth, surfing on the waves underneath. I understood then.

Drowning

Ayen led me down a carpeted aisle, further into the temple. The room opened into a cathedral ceiling with a checkered floor and rows of benches. We passed under a large chandelier that swung over the center of the room like a pendulum. He led me past the center podium and through a door, to a small room in the back. The other Architects were praying and meditating in a circle.

"Hello brothers," Ayen said loudly as he walked in. "Time for class."

"No," I protested, immediately. "I need to see Jeeny."

"There's no time," Ayen said. "You have a duty to do."

"I can't," I argued. "She's not safe."

"None of us are, so take a seat."

"No!" I yelled.

"You have to!" He yelled back, pointing at a mat for me to sit on.

"I'll go find her," said Zane, standing up. He looked at Ayen, who nodded to confirm.

"Thank you," I said.

"She's at the loading docks," Zane said, optimistically. He quickly left the room.

"Right!" Ayen boomed."To business, shall we?"

"First," Ode started, "this is a bicameral government."

"What does that mean?" I asked.

"I told you we're all screwed," Ayen joked.

"Just remember it, okay?" Ode said. "It's the legislative branch, but the importance is to focus on the process of legislation."

"You shined a spotlight on the door of the

parliament and formed a service that allowed anyone to step into the light," riddled Ayen.

"It gave much prestige to the members of parliament who judged the laws. They communicated more with the public," said Ode. "A lot of people liked it."

"We still don't trust them, though," said Keith. A faint laugh passed around the room.

"Continue," Ayen directed.

"From there," said Ode, "the politics of Avalon were easily accessible by the citizens. Policies, actions and regulations followed suit and allowed the efficient progress and design of this nation. We were led by great thinkers and, after the first few years, the country thrived economically. After establishing financial independence, the nation broke away from its original investors and established its own currency under the ideal that the value of money is worthless, unless bereft of motivation."

"I'm not really understanding this," I said.

"You'll remember it when you need it," said another Architect.

"You practically killed money," Ayen said. "That's why you died."

"Nice to know," I lied sarcastically. "I still have no idea how to do this."

"You won't do it alone," said Ode. "Many will help you from all over the world."

"How?" I asked.

"You will," Ode replied.

"The will," Ayen corrected. "Just stay open and focused."

"Okay," I said.

They explained to me how important observing the truth in nature was; that what happens outside, is reflecting what's happening inside and this is all an experiment dealing with the soul. Everything unites in perpetual division – the holy trinity, they said. I didn't understand, but I wanted to and kept listening. They said we will defeat time and space. I couldn't comprehend.

Ayen, after the lecture, walked me out to the front.

"You'll have enough time to see Jeeny," he said.

"Thanks," I replied. "Where do I go?"

"Go back the way you came, you'll run into her and Zane," he rhymed.

"How do you know?" I asked.

"Didn't you hear the rhyme? Damn, boy, they don't come in disguise," he joked. I laughed.

"Thanks!" I smiled and turned away down the stairs.

"Hail to the King!" He yelled as I ran down the street.

~~~

"Alef!" I heard her beautiful call slice through the air. It was Jeeny. The ground rumbled and a loud crack echoed across the land. She ran into my arms. Zane was behind her.

"I got him!" He yelled out. His right eye was black and he had blood smeared across his cheek.

"Are you okay?" I asked.

"Yeah," he said, still catching his breath. "I distracted him, she ran. It worked out for her, not so much for me." He laughed about it. I laughed too.

"Thanks Zane," I said.

"No problem."

"What are you guys doing at the temple?" I asked him.

"We're going back," he said.
~~~

"Back?"

"Yeah," he replied.

"Where?"

"Time. Space. Source."

"How?"

"We didn't build this temple just for show," Zane laughed. "It's a boat."

"How?"

"I can't say." He paused for a moment. "I'll leave you notes throughout history," he said, smiling to himself. "Goodbye you two." He reached out his hand.

"Thanks," I said shaking it. He smiled.

He turned to Jeeny and she hugged him.

"Goodbye," she said.

"Stay in school," he said, looking both of us before turning around. He quickly ran off back towards the temple.

I held Jeeny tightly.

"We should get you out of here," I said to her.

"What about you?"

I ignored the question as she led me towards the rail system. She started sobbing as we made our way down the stairs to the underground train.

"You have to go back, don't you?" She cried.

"Yes," I said, staring at the ground as I walked.

"How?" She asked

"I don't know," I lied.

"I want to go with you."

"You can't," I denied.

"I have to," she insisted.

"You can't!" I yelled, turning to her, tears filling my eyes. "You're just a dream!"

"I know," she sobbed. "I'd rather be a dream than lost in time without you."

I pulled her close and pushed the button. We held each other in silence for a moment.

"You know where to go?" I asked her.

"Yes." She nodded and hugged me close.

Ding.

The door to the box opened and we entered. She hit a button on the side panel and a burst of air shot out from the bottom. A screen on the wall screamed red showing many of the transport locations were already under water. Not our route. The doors closed.

"Ready?"

~~~

We held each other close, listening to our pounding hearts slow down and synchronize. Five minutes of this melancholic peace passed.

Ding.

The silver doors opened to another staircase. We held hands up the stairs to a door. Jeeny opened it and led me down a dim-lit cement path. We were walking around a building. I followed closely behind her. We walked up to the front door and she opened it. We entered and I immediately recognized where we were. In the center of the room was a giant silver funnel.

"Why here?" I asked.

"The eruption was on the opposite side of Avalon," she said. "I'm hoping this gives us the most time together." I smiled and pulled her close.

The ground started shaking and loud booms erupted underneath as the land oscillated in agony.

Jeeny let go and disappeared into the cafeteria room, returning to her food cart. I looked out the window, but couldn't see anything.
~~~

"The stew is still hot!" She yelled out to me.

"Fix me one, please!" I shouted back.

A minute passed and she came back with two bowls full of stew and a thick piece of bread drowning in each.

"Thanks, dear," I said.

"You're welcome," she replied. "Let's go outside."

"Okay."

The ground rumbled again and started to shift.

"This stew is delicious," I said to her as we made our way through the door into the fresh, salty air.

"Thanks," she said, taking the bread out and biting into it.

The ground slowly bubbled.

"Won't be long now," I said.

"Look at that!" Jeeny pointed towards the center of Avalon. A bright light flew out from the center of Camelot. It quickly darted up, then turned, burning over the sinking nation – watching.

"Usually stars land, instead of take off," I laughed.

We finished our soup and held each other close, watching the star recede into the sky.

"Ayen left a note for me on the stew," she whispered. "He knew I would stay with you." Her arms tightened around me. "Forever."

The ground let out a giant crack and started to rise.

"No!" I screamed.

"Get to the back!" She yelled, grabbing my hand and leading me around the building. "We're going to ride this as much as we can!"

The rear of the building sloped so we could easily walk up the side. We found a nice vantage point on top next to the funnel.

We held hands for a minute in silent horror, watching the world fade away in awe.

The ground quickly lunged up. Jeeny screamed. Her arms squeezed around me as the island shook. The lights from Camelot in the distance grew faint and disappeared as Avalon succumbed to the ocean. The ground beneath us rose higher and higher to the sky, cracking and wrenching upwards from the pressure. The air turned salty as the land slipped deeper into the ocean, turning upwards and away from its inevitable fate into the waters. To no avail.

The funnel hut cracked and shook. It was in its death throes.

“I won't forget you, my Queen.”

“I'll hold you forever, my King.”

The building lunged out from underneath us. I held Jeeny as tight as I could and we fell.

www.ingramcontent.com/pod-product-compliance
Ingram Content Group UK Ltd.
Pitfield, Milton Keynes, MK11 3LW, UK
UKHW020238250726
13967UKWH00001B/429

9 781304 358387